Earth, My Body

Poems by

Richard Sievers

Earth, My Body

First Addition

Text copyright © 2010 Richard Sievers

Cover Paintings copyright © 2009 Richard Sievers

All rights reserved.

No part of this book may be reproduced in any manner without written permission from the author except in the case of brief quotations embodied in reviews and articles.

e-mail:

fieldofsevenhouses@yahoo.com

Because of the dynamic nature of the internet, any web addresses contained in this book may have changed since publication and may no longer be valid.

Field of Seven Houses Publishing

ISBN: 978-0-9829207-0-1

In memory of

Robbie, Janine, and the Island I once called home.

With gratitude to

My family, my community: People of the Heart, and the Spirits who whisper in the prairie grasses and sing on the ocean's hidden highways.

Earth my body
   Water my blood
      Air my breath
         And fire my spirit

Old Pagan Chant

Contents

Old Apple Tree	9
Ten Billion Years	10
Everyday, Everywhere, Everyone	12
Dreamer, the Winged Have No Hands	13
The Desert	14
Floating out the Window	16
Mountain, River, Bed	18
Heart of the Ocean	20
Did You See?	21
Don't Go Back to Sleep	22
Driving through the Woodland	24
Addiction to Heaven	25
Let the Song for the Trees Be Your Offering	26
Writing the Veins	28
Bury My Heart at Sea	29
Forest Fire	30
Oil Spill Lament	31
Today, after the Storm	32
Summer Swelter	34
Holy Things	36
Twilight	38
What If	40
Enetai	42
Kneeling at the Altar	44
Stones I and II	46
Garden Prayer	48
Sleepless	49
Revisiting the Grave	50
About Rick: Writing Desk Window	51

Old Apple Tree

Two ravens call to me
and circle the sun.
I rise through
shimmering branches.
No thoughts.
No reasons.
The dancing of the branches,
the swaying of the fruit,
the working of the winds...
                these are real.

Ten Billion Years

Ten billion years before
I touched you
we were particles
from a dozen blazing suns
now dark. Our puzzle
pieces were hidden
within planets
hung on sound
strings, exploding
in the electric blue mind
of the Great Song.

Brought here now,
you and me, entering
the enveloping
midnight of breath
and bone behind
the star shine of eyes.

So many births
for this moment,
fitting together,
proton and electron,
nova and satellite,
infinite pieces shifted
from primal energy.

Let us be
one more exploding sun,
one more burning nebula.
Let us explore the secrets
of the universe once more.

Everyday, Everywhere, Everyone

Remember this.
We walk
upon the graves
of our ancestors,
and the creatures now shy
of sun and sound.
Everywhere we tread
a life has been borne.
All of the sleepers
once like us.
I wonder if they feel
me walking above
their stony beds?
I wonder if I will
make my patient descent
into the grass with ease?
Will it be lonely,
the time after today,
when I hear the footsteps
above my empty chest?
Who remains?
Who waits for me
in the secret world?

Dreamer, the Winged Have No Hands

Would you exchange
your hands
for wings?
What loss comes
with flight?
What joy
with soaring?

Why do angels
have both
fingers and feathers?

Why must we
choose one
or the other?

The Desert

The desert is singing for you,
there, within the cutting spines
and dried drowning of mudflows,
there beneath the white bones and
wasted lives, shining in
the broken wine bottles and
spent casings.

I am the parched lips whispering to
you, brother, sister.
My voice is a gift:
"Just let it out. Set it to the wind,
all the broken wings and bones.
Everything is holy now.
We are the Spirits,
with their love,
and their tears,
in the mess and
the sunrise after
misunderstanding.
I am holy now.
I am everything out there.
So are you."
Feel the sand beneath
your feet, there by the ants
who make their way on hidden
highways and impossible errands.

Let the grains pass,
praising each one.
No more or less
important than each
word on your precious
white pages.
Release the stories
into the wind. They
come as they are,
just like you,
imperfect and holy.
Your angers,
and their discomfort.
Your soaring poems
and their melodies of heart.

It's dawn.
The coffee eyelids of
sunrise give
way to the bright egg
cracked wide open.

You don't have to be
nice, or good.
Just be
another shining thing
in the desert, breathing
your particular life,
your one holy life.

Floating out the Window

A jet plane is wheeling
through the high
cloud bank like a leaf
bouncing down
a great grey river.

At that height the pilots
already see
the ocean I can only feel.

Through my window,
set in its crooked frame,
above the field where
the robins play,
here is my earth.

I am sparkling
in spirals and floating
out through the window

The pilots are at the controls.
They gaze out the windshield
of their fragile craft.

Their diamond lights cover
a wide trajectory of sight,
yet hold no more wonder
than this cabin's pane.

Flying high or falling
in love with the ordinary,
it's all the same.

How good it is to live!
How good it is
to witness what is right,
here close to the dewy
grass, bent with the lucky
burden of growth.

Mountain, River, Bed

You've carved
a well-worn river
bed into my arm.
In this dry season
the channel is deep and ragged,
full of thoughts and memory.
When the rain falls
on your distant mountains
I become full of your eyes
shining, my love.
Flood me,
my dark
mountain fairy.
Flood me
again.
~~~
~~
~

From your lodge
on the dark mountain,
where I cannot go,
speak to me softly.
Let the cloud's night fall
from your mouth.
Shatter the sky
with my name.
Cry above this world,
down canyons
of carved skin.
In this desert place,
send one word,
my name,
sung in the rain,
my name,
written in the flood,
quenching
this bright
dry
season.

~~~

~~

~

Heart of the Ocean

I love you
in the deepest
heart of the ocean,
beneath the waves
beyond the sun, buried
in the crystal embers
of trembling power,
in a bed where dreams are
not just dreams anymore.
I love you
in the dark,
knowing nothing but
the hum of currents,
leaving, arriving, spiraling
in this place beneath
the world, with no words or body,
nothing but you, beyond
the storms and sun, floating
above the womb
of the earth, born
moment to moment
by unseen hands and fingers.
I love you
here forever
in the dark
heart of the ocean.

Did You See?

Did you see the crescent moon,
the dark sphere held in
the silver cup?

I am free.

Did you see how small I am,
so fragile,
so in love
with the moon?

Don't Go Back to Sleep

I woke before dawn,
a thrumming whistle
in my head.
Awakened by the
song of my mortality.
Awakened by the universe
singing:
> *Don't go back to sleep.*
> *Come to the shoreline*
> *of your yearnings and*
> *dive right in.*

All the dangerous
years of living nice
were washed off
like the skin
off the soul.

I once hid my bones
in a coffin of smiles
to keep the vexed ones
at a distance.
Now I sleep with
the vexed.
Now I hide from
the song of myself.

Now I hear the throb
of eternity in
my arteries.
> *Don't go back to sleep*
> *Don't go back to sleep*

Driving Through the Woodland

Out there:
the long shadows
and the red sun leaf falling
upon the field,
frost on the blueberry,
tangled dogwood sparkling
molecular star fields.
Out there, the moments
of silence between the cars
and the dogs barking.
Sky blue as your eyes,
wide as the net
of your praise,
the wind, a song
rushing through your fingers

Addiction to Heaven

How I needed
the grand staircase
to paradise,
the drama of ecstasy,
the denial and oblivion,
the drug of someday.
God's cells wept
within my body.
How I needed the fix
of somewhere better
until I came to you,
wife with dirt under your fingernails,
hair strewn grey as
the wintry dome of morning,
eyes watching a fool who was
dismissing this world,
trying to climb into heaven
when it had fallen in heaps
all around him.

Let the Song for the Trees Be Your Offering

Out across the quiet field,
the wild cherry remembers
the song she sprouted from.
She wears the happiness of winter
with her white robe folded
around her wrinkled body.

What joy when clothed
with swirling stars!
What joy when vestments
fall, flooding
the meadow with
petals of manna!

Two robins bring moss
to the crook of her canopy,
building a nest and
hope on a limb
into summer.
They weave dreams
of their children
through her branches.

Holy, the benediction
of procreation.
Holy, the baptism
of shedding all hindrance
to Summer light.

The blooms
lean into the sun,
releasing their brilliance,
trading their treasure
for the soft dappled gathering
of buds in heady summer breezes.

Spirit Wind,
blow your light
into new galaxies.
Mother Earth,
pull down the sunlight
onto your stretching loam.
Brother Star,
shine within the secret
rings of the heartwood.
Sister Rain,
remember our thirst
for any news of the sea.

Writing the Veins

What if I wrote
the veins
write out
of my skin?

Red and blue,
the map
of longing displayed
for everyone
to see,
the reflection
of a hundred thousand
tributaries melding
into the
horizon.

I'd pull my face
up from the desk
to see the wide land.

I might even stumble
into the meadow, singing
into the new world,
free to rest,
free for the first time
once again.

Bury My Heart at Sea

Bury my heart
at sea, where its secrets
spread into the
diffuse dark
of the waters.

Every word never
spoken, all the cowering
in fear of the roar
of blood and breath,
all the secret scripts,
are laid down
between the waves,
sculpting the sieve
of the sand.

These are the tokens
of failure, offerings
to life hoped for.
These are the
human gifts given
for the silver
of the moon and
the song of the sun.
These are the trinkets
of longing handed over
for the gold that rises
with the morning.

Forest Fire
The Castle Rock Complex in Central Idaho
August 2007

Something has been released.
Something has been taken.
Something has been offered.
A part of the body cries. A wisp
of hope hovers in mid-air, gasping
for earth. An old wooden
span has snapped.
The house, once shiny,
moans on her foundations.
Do you feel the pressure plummet?
An opening for the storm drops in
from the desert through the charred flanks
of once glacial rivulets.
The house knows her fate from the creaking
of the ceiling and the shuddering
of panes and jams.
Prepare ye the way for Holy Karma,
Destroyer, Creator
of changing winds,
lover of smoky offerings.

Oil Spill Lament

The sun comes, and
then goes. The rivers
fall into the sea,
which rises into
the eyes of God.

The Great One cries
a healing song
upon His bride
the Earth… the one
the people of the book
call *Cursed*.

Today, after the Storm

Today I will
gaze upon the field.
I will
do the work of watching,
remembering reverently
the wild night
we passed through.

I will
be free to know stillness.
I will
be more than happy
and less than sad.

See the single scarlet
leaf, maple's last flutter
of Autumn's song.

Hear the crystal
bowl of earth
ripple within the sun streams.

Touch the frosted
footfalls, weaving
tales of last night
into the grasses.

Daylight has come.

The curling fist
of the storm
is now an open
hand unwound.
Pull the blinds.
Invite your eyes
into the wide and blue.

The people can wait.
The chores and sweat can wait.
The doings will rest.
The field is enough.

Summer Swelter

It's a day steeped in flames
where the rusty dog no longer barks,
where the tap tap tap of the sprinkler
offers its reward as a song from childhood.
It's the hot of shuttered houses,
the hot of once bright clothes bleached
pale and limp on the clothesline.
The burning eye of smoke from the dying forest
is a drug in the paralyzed dream of the afternoon.
The boiling moon rises in ripples unquenched.
All the creatures panting in faint breaths
come down the canyons in search of the withering pond.

Draped beside the apple tree,
my love observes a cooler country
on the other side
of the sun. She gazes up
through branches heavy with fruit,
her hand anchored to the back of my neck.
Sweat conducts lightning between our skin.
Smoke rises as she strokes up the moon,
her burning fingers trembling in my hair.

Holy Things

Holy things show
themselves through surprise.

Like the island rising
over the shoulder of the road
when I was lost.

Your glowing
face at the airport
curb.

This white farmhouse
I'd passed by
for years.

A poem tipping over
the edge of dawn, before
the newspaper hit the driveway.

The perfume of the river
as we flew our open
windows across the bridge.

Sunlight spearing
through the crystal
on our breakfast table.

A covey of quail
in the quivering
snowberry.

The foghorn
I heard two hundred
miles from the sea.

The home I dreamed
of moments before
I woke in your arms.

Twilight

Bright eye moon, veiled in
the spinning wool of clouds.
Vapors hissing and burning
at sunset. Rain drops,
heavy with yesterday's trade winds,
falling upon our windshield.

We sat in the car,
shedding the snake skin
of our mountain road.
Sky flinging her scarlet
hair. Her whispering tunes
dancing in the winds.
Her rising breath weaving
through the shaking trees.

We took photo after photo
through the side window, trying
to collect the light and rain.
Then the scrutiny of the lens was put
away. We held hands.
Held our breath. We lifted
right out of the gaping windows.

Our lives as we knew them
were over. The fortress
of clouds falling all around us.
The ramparts melting.
Our home revealed
through the silence
beyond walls.

Perhaps this is too holy
to explain here.

There are moments
when heaven becomes earth,
when lovers become
sun-spun vapors of twilight.
Spirits.
Not quite separate anymore.
Quiet.
The horizon alive with
ruby flames shimmering
through the waves
of ridge stone and mountain fir.

What If

What if there was a middle way
between the trinkets of consuming and
the sacrifice of selflessness?
Could everyone's needs be met?
What if you were so humble in spirit
that you woke up
to inherit the world?

What if you trusted your heart,
opened your mind
and spoke with your own voice?
What if you wrote
a prayer with your life,
held the hand of the Earth's
gift to you,
lived prosperously,
gave easily,
breathed deeply,
slept deeply,
created richly?

Look, the sky is blazing blue
between the clouds and geese wheeling.
The sun and rain are dancing together.
The corn is welling sweet with honey.
The cat is asleep at your feet.
All is as it should be.
You've come this far.
Now, step through the clouds.

The sun is gold in the corn.
Last night's rain is glistening
like a million stars.

Enetai

A Northwest Native term meaning:
To cross from one side to another

Tonight
wisdom's whisper
rises from
the roaming tides:

"An island
is really
just a mountain.

The sea fills
in the air
between
here and there.

The land
runs hidden
between us.

There is
no real
separation.

There are
highways and fields
beneath the waves."

I cross over
the water
like flying

Kneeling at the Altar

At the Hermitage of Christian Brothers
above the Chama River, New Mexico.

I lit a candle long and tallow white.
I lit my head on fire,
then placed it deep in your tray
of Chama's sand,
melting with the river's song.
I lit the forest of all of my ideas,
watched them burn,
cold fire, blue suns,
red eyes of stone,
blazing, melting, smoking.
The basalt in my chest
bubbling and frothing up
the charnel rapids,
right into your altar,
where I lit a candle,
where I placed the last small stone held
from a home I will never live in again,
where I put my shaking
dollar leaf into the golden coffer
and let it burn, let it drift into smoke.

I am the grinding of the channel
full of the sun's diamonds,
rising in fins and wavelets.
I am the checkered cliff body
whose feet slump into the
vetch and willow.
I am the long winding grove
of scrub oak bowing
in worship to the southern way.
I am a blink of a thought,
a neuron firing in the mind.
I am a spark, a coal,
and the resurrection of my
dead solidity, resurrected
into the sun's arms.

I am yours, Mother.
Do with me what you will.

The cold blue ocean
of your eyes, cleansing me,
moving me homeward, down
to the shores of my life,
and all the breaths left for me.
Here on earth as it is in heaven.
Holy Mother,
sacred world, vespers of starlight,
tumbling stones,
O Sweet Fire in my head.

Stones I and II

I. Seven Tons
Building a Stone Wall

The stone people are coming!
We'll be lifting their spirits.
Placing their hard
bodies into the soil.
Five hundred hearts of the planet
falling onto the hungry earth
that will swallow them whole,
pulling their songs back
into the darkness where
they were born.

II. Offering Stone
Given before an Ocean Voyage

I found a stone with a mouth
that told stories of falling into the sun.
The stone had eyes glittering
with a map of the dark earth's riches.
My hand held the stone.
The stone held my soul.
We left all other maybe lovers behind,
spinning into the wild calm,
sinking, shining and drunk,
down through the dark pearl sea,
into a warm lap, a blanket of stars
and a thousand songs
waiting to be remembered.

Garden Prayer

Walk with me, Beloved.
Make this garden like the first.
Let me hold your hand and kiss your face.
Let the animals lie beside us as we ponder rain drops.
Let us share the sweet fruits of the happily laden tree.
Let us laugh with a joyous joke that only we understand.
Be with me in the garden, Beloved.
Let us love unashamed.
Let me wipe your tears away.
Let me name the deer you raised in the woodland.
Let me sow in the clay from which you made me.
Let us worship love as we look into each other's eyes.
Walk with me in the sunlit garden…
                this innocence like the first.

Sleepless

Watching Orion
rising at 2am.
O, what terrible
beauty...
the consolation
for being
awake.

Revisiting the Grave

Your stone grove
is a cold song
of forest shadows.
No heat there.
No heart.
Only the forever
of changing tides
clinging to the skirts
of your island.

How far I've come
from our sea.

Tell me,
in whispers.
How can my life be
a *Yes* today?
How do I breathe in
the blazing world
before the cool clay of earth
becomes my home too?
How do I sing
the secrets
of the ocean
in a dry and rocky land?

Writing Desk Window

Now the field is
an ocean of light.
The spirals are
eddies and whirlpools.
Frozen time
is thawed.
I am islands
and desert spires.
I am the sleeper
awakened.
I am the spirits
of mountain stone.
I am the window and
I am the grasses.

Rick is a poet, artist, builder, ordained minister, and part-time farmer. He lives with his family on the remnant of an old Finnish farm in southwest Washington State.

Rick's websites:
www.fieldofsevehouses.com
www.fieldofsevenhouses.blogspot.com

www.ingramcontent.com/pod-product-compliance
Lightning Source LLC
Chambersburg PA
CBHW031433040426
42444CB00006B/791